ELLIOTT CARTER

GLOCK BIRTHDAY FANFARE

for 3 Trumpets and Vibraphone (Chimes)

This fanfare opened and closed a British Broadcasting program of verbal tributes by many musicians, including Elliott Carter, celebrating the 70th birthday of Sir William Glock, BBC's Controller of Music

AMP 8136
First Printing: May 1998

ISBN No. 0-7935-9158-9

Associated Music Publishers, Inc.

for Sir William Glock's 70th (May 3, 1978)

GLOCK BIRTHDAY FANFARE

Elliott Carter

Brisk, ♩ = ca. 72

Trumpets in C 1 2 3

Vibraphone (Chimes)

* Passages enclosed in brackets (⌐ ¬) should be brought out.

Trumpet 1 in C

for Sir William Glock's 70th (May 3, 1978)

GLOCK BIRTHDAY FANFARE

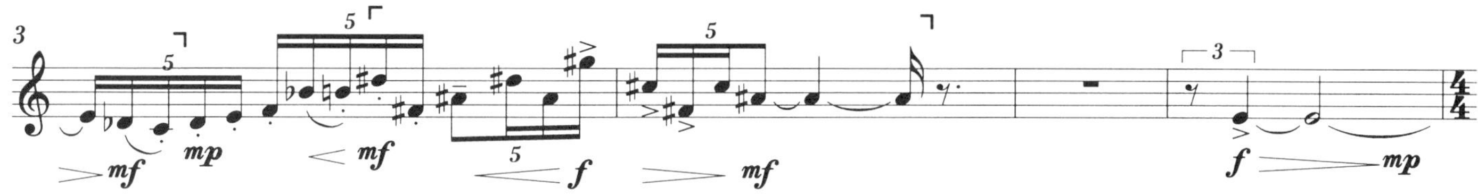

* Passages enclosed in brackets (⌐ ¬) should be brought out.

** From here to the end, the three trumpets should be equally balanced.

Trumpet 2 in C

for Sir William Glock's 70th (May 3, 1978)

GLOCK BIRTHDAY FANFARE

Elliott Carter

* Passages enclosed in brackets (⌐ ¬) should be brought out.
** From here to the end, the three trumpets should be equally balanced.

Trumpet 3 in C

for Sir William Glock's 70th (May 3, 1978)

GLOCK BIRTHDAY FANFARE

Elliott Carter

Brisk, ♩ = ca. 72

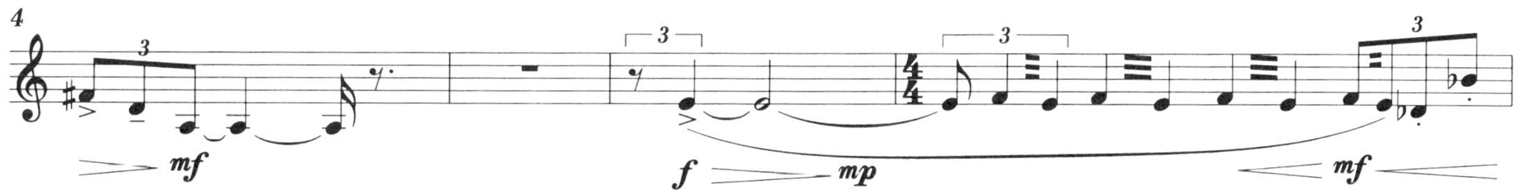

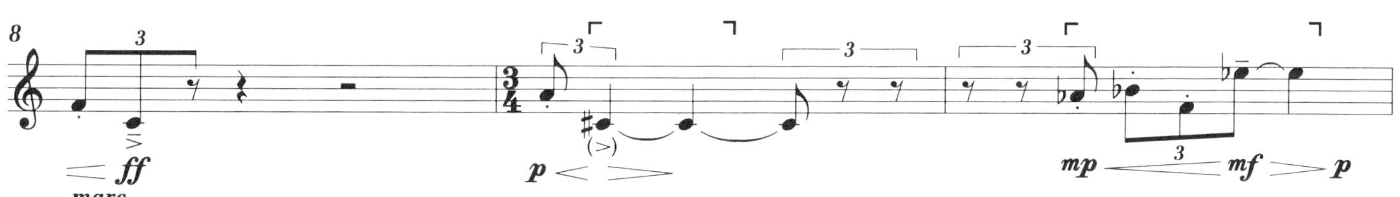

* Passages enclosed in brackets (⌐ ¬) should be brought out.

** From here to the end, the three trumpets should be equally balanced.

Vibraphone
(Chimes)

for Sir William Glock's 70th (May 3, 1978)

GLOCK BIRTHDAY FANFARE

Elliott Carter

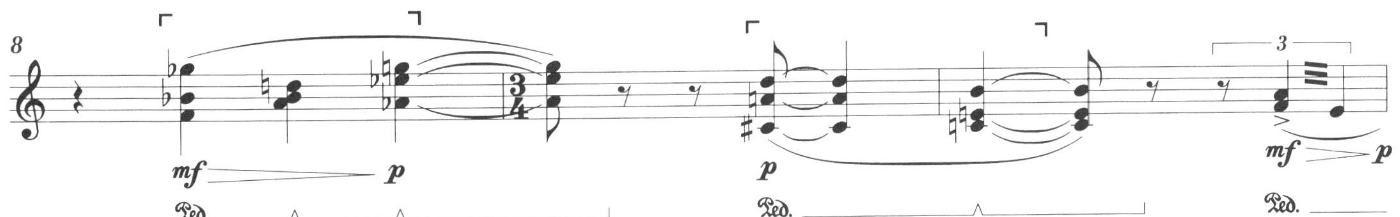

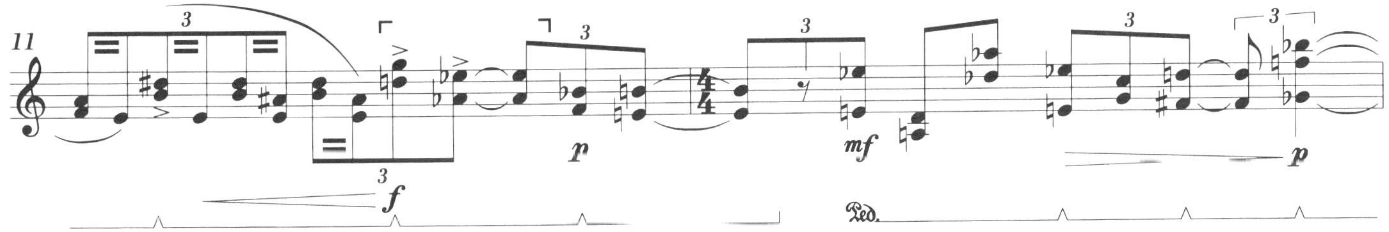

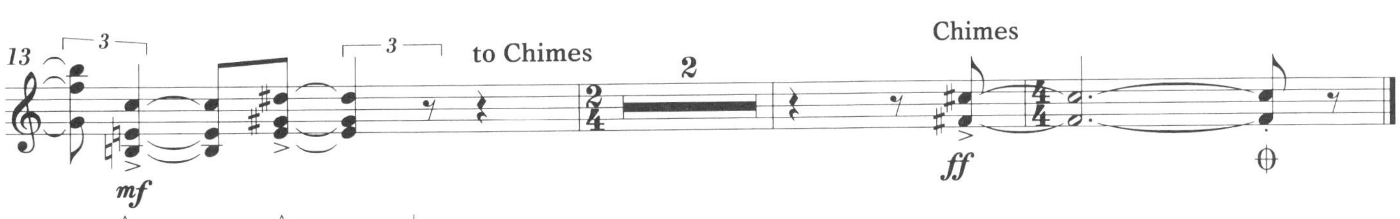

* Passages enclosed in brackets (⌐ ¬) should be brought out.

* From here to the end, the three trumpets should be equally balanced.